BUTTERFL[Y]

PATTERNS ON PAGE 2[0]
Perch this charming creature on your straw so you see it every time you take a drink.

- Art foam (9" x 12" sheets):
  - 1 purple (cut 1 Butterfly B)
  - 1 yellow (cut 2 Wing B's)
  - 1 chartreuse green (cut 2 Wing C's)
- Gold glitter dimensional paint
- Drinking straw

Glue wing designs onto butterfly. Use a knife to cut two slits to insert straw into butterfly. Outline each wing with glitter paint.

[D]AISY-FLY [A]RRANGEMENT

[P]ATTERNS ON PAGES 20 & 23
[T]hese move when the wind blows! Stick them right in the dirt of [y]our garden or flowerbed, or put sand in a flowerpot and then stick [th]em in that.

[F]or 6 daisies and 6 butterflies]

Art foam (9" x 12" sheets):

- 1 white (cut 6 Daisies)
- 1 chartreuse green (cut 1 Butterfly C, 2 Wing A's, 2 Heart A's, 6 Daisy Backs, and 12 Leaves)
- 1 yellow (cut 1 Butterfly C, 2 Wing A's, 2 Heart A's, and 6 Daisy Centers)
- 1 pink (cut 1 Butterfly C, 2 Wing A's, and 2 Heart A's)
- 1 purple (cut 1 Butterfly C, 2 Wing A's, and 2 Heart A's)
- 1 orange (cut 1 Butterfly C, 2 Wing A's, and 2 Heart A's)
- 1 blue (cut 1 Butterfly C, 2 Wing A's, and 2 Heart A's)
- 1 black (cut 12 Thorax A's)

24-gauge green pre-cut floral wire 14" in length

Gold glitter dimensional paint

[G]lue daisy center to daisy. Glue floral wire to center back of daisy [a]s stem. Glue daisy back over end of wire. Poke wire into flat end [o]f leaf twice and push up. Use marker to add leaf and daisy petal [li]nes. Lay floral wire on body area and glue a butterfly over it. Glue [a] thorax on other side. Glue on hearts and wings, let them dry, and [o]utline them with gold glitter.

FAIRY CROWN

PATTERNS ON PAGE 20 & 23
Wearing this makes it easy to pretend you're a fairy! Boy fairies wear crowns too, but without the ribbons.

- Art foam (9" x 12" sheets):
  - 1 pink (cut 4 Butterfly A's)
  - 1 orange (cut 1 Star B)
  - 1 yellow (cut 1 Star B)
  - 1 purple (cut 2 Star B's)
- 1 yard ⅛" ribbon: orange satin, yellow satin, pink satin, and purple grosgrain
- 1 yard of ⅝" yellow/orange butterfly print satin ribbon
- Gold glitter dimensional paint
- Wired cording or tinsel

Outline each butterfly in gold glitter dimensional paint. Measure wired cording or tinsel around head and twist ends together to form a circle. Alternate gluing butterflies and stars onto circle, using clothespins until glue dries. Loop and secure ribbons onto circle.

BUTTERFLY PENCIL FAVOR

PATTERNS ON PAGE 20

This perky butterfly on a pencil is a great gift to make for your friends or give as a favor at your next party.

- Art foam (9" x 12" sheets):
  - 1 pink (cut 1 Butterfly C)
  - 1 purple (cut 2 Wing A's and 2 Heart A's)
- Gold glitter dimensional paint
- Pencil
- 14" of 1/8" ribbon:
  - Orange satin
  - Yellow satin
  - Pink satin
  - Purple grosgrain
  - Yellow picot satin

Glue wings and hearts on butterfly. Use a knife to cut two lines for pencil insertion. Outline wings and hearts with glitter paint. Tie ribbon on pencil.

BUTTERFLY NAPKIN RING

PATTERNS ON PAGE 20

Next time you set the table, use these attractive butterfly napkin rings! They're fun to make, and sure to please everyone who uses them.

[For 1 napkin ring]
- Art foam (9" x 12" sheets):
  - 1 white (napkin ring base)
  - 1 white (cut 1 Butterfly C)
  - 1 green (cut 2 Wing A's and 2 Heart A's)
  - 1 black (cut 1 Thorax A)
- Gold glitter dimensional paint

Glue ends of base together so they overlap 1". Use clothespins until dry. Glue thorax, hearts, and wings onto butterfly. Outline edges of wings and hearts with glitter paint. Glue ring to back of butterfly.

BUTTERFLY MASK

PATTERNS ON PAGE 20 & 31

Use the bold colors and patterns shown or study some butterflies on your own and adapt the project to match them.

- Art foam (9" x 12" sheets):
  - 1 (12" x 18" sheet) lavender (cut 1 Butterfly Mask on fold, so it creates an entire butterfly)
  - 1 green glitter (cut 2 Heart C's)
  - 1 gold glitter (cut 2 Heart E's)
  - 1 blue glitter (cut 2 Heart E's)
  - 1 purple glitter (cut 2 Heart E's)
  - 1 fuchsia glitter (cut 2 Heart D's)
  - 1 black glitter (cut 1 Thorax C)
- Dimensional paint: gold glitter
- 3" of gold metallic chenille stem
- 2 wood tongue depressors

Cut out heart openings on butterfly as marked. Glue on thorax and hearts. Cut one tongue depressor to 4¼" and glue to back of butterfly. Glue other tongue depressor below the first, extending at least 3" below body. Use gold glitter to add dots and swirls.

SPARKLY CHAIN

is chain is so easy to make and so fun to use! You can wear it
ound your neck or hang it on furniture or plants to brighten a
om.

Glitter art foam:

• ¾" x 4½" strips from various colors

ue the ends of one strip together to form a loop. Use clothespins
til dry. Insert next strip through loop and glue so loops chain
gether. Repeat until chain is as long as you want it.

TAR PURSE

TTERNS ON PAGES 23 & 32

e only thing better than carrying a sparkly star purse like this one
making it yourself!

Art foam:

• 1 (9" x 12" sheet) purple glitter (cut 2 Purse A's)

• 2 gold glitter stars (2¼" pre-cut or cut Star C's)

• 4 gold glitter stars (1" pre-cut or cut Star A's)

1 yard of ¹⁄₁₆" lavender sparkly silky cord

1" piece of Velcro

ferring to pattern, use paper punch to make holes approximately
" from outside edge. Adhere 2 small stars and 1 large star to each
itter side. Use silky cord and go in and out of punched holes to
e the sections together. Glue cord ends to inside. Cut a 1" x 11"
ip from purple glitter and glue for handle; use clothespins until
y. Glue Velcro to top edge on each inside section in center.

FAIRY WAND

PATTERN ON PAGE 23

Next time you take a walk, use this wand to touch a leaf or flower
and save a fairy. Pay close attention and maybe you'll see a fairy,
small animal, or other fun surprise!

• Art foam (9" x 12" sheet): gold glitter (cut 2 Star D's)

• Drinking straw

• 18" of ¹⁄₈" ribbon:

  • Orange satin

  • Yellow satin

  • Pink satin

  • Purple grosgrain

Glue straw between backs of two stars. Tie ribbons onto straw.

CROWN

PATTERNS ON PAGES 23 & 32

King, Queen, Prince, or Princess—this crown is fit for them all. Make one for each member of your family and let them choose which gems they want.

- 1 (9" x 12" sheet) gold glitter art foam (cut 1 Crown and 1 Star A)
- 3½" strip of Velcro
- Various styles of rhinestones, buttons, and bows

Cut a 1¾" x 10" strip from gold glitter foam and glue to one side of crown. Use clothespins until dry. On other end glue one section of Velcro. Glue remaining section of Velcro to crown. This will help determine the size needed to fit the wearer. Glue star to top of center point. Glue on rhinestones, buttons, and bows as desired.

BIBLE BOOKMARK

PATTERNS ON PAGE 21

This special bookmark will help you keep your place in your Bible or other book.

- Art foam (9" x 12" sheets):
  - 1 yellow (cut 1 Bookmark)
  - 1 fuchsia glitter (cut 1 Cross)
- 2" tan, white, or yellow tassel
- Acrylic paint:
  - Royal Fuchsia
  - Lamp Black

Glue cross into upper half of bookmark. Paint a broken line in Royal Fuchsia around outer edge of bookmark. Use Lamp Black to paint "Keep your place with God" onto lower half of bookmark. Once dry, repeat for opposite side, if desired. Use hole punch to make a hole ¼" from top center edge. Place tassel end into hole and through loop.

OFFERING PURSE

PATTERNS ON PAGES 21 & 32

This purse will help you remember to carry your money to church.

- Art foam (9" x 12" sheets):
  - 1 turquoise (cut 2 Purse B's)
  - 1 yellow (cut 2 Crosses)
- 1⅛ yard yellow picot satin ribbon
- 1" Velcro (sticky on both sides)
- ⅝" foam sticker letters
- Gold glitter foam paint or pen

KEEP
YOUR
PLACE
WITH
GOD

Glue a cross to each purse piece. Glue each end of a 12" piece of ribbon to inner side of one piece for handle. Glue purse pieces together, leaving top edge open. Remove paper from both sides of Velcro. Position one sticky side on inside of purse and then press sides of purse together to adhere the other side. Use white quick-dry glue to attach ribbon ⅜" from top edge and bottom edge. Outline cross with gold glitter. Let dry completely and repeat on other side. Place the letters "GOD" on front cross. Tie remaining picot ribbon into a bow and glue to center of back cross.

TAR NECKLACE

ATTERN ON PAGE 23

s stylish necklace is easy to make. Perfect for any star!

1 (9" x 12" sheet) gold glitter art foam (cut 1 Star C)

24" of 1/16" lilac sparkly silky cord

e a hole punch to make a hole in two star points vertically across
m each other. Thread cording through from back of star. Tie a
it at end of cording.

TAR BRACELET

TTERNS ON PAGE 23

essorize your wardrobe with this bracelet! Use the stars, as
wn, or substitute hearts, butterflies, or some other shape.

foam (9" x 12" sheets):

- 1 gold glitter (cut 5 or 6 Star A's)
- 1 green glitter (cut 2 Star B's)
- 1 purple (cut 1 Star B)

Gold metallic chenille stem or wired gold metallic tinsel/cording
(length depends on size of wrist)

asure wrist and cut chenille, tinsel, or cording 1" longer than that.
ist the ends together to form a circle, making sure the bracelet is
t too tight. Glue stars onto circle and use clothespins until dry.

STAR RING

PATTERNS ON PAGE 23

The magical powers of this ring are available only to the one who
wears it. Be gone and create!

- Art foam (9" x 12" sheets):
  - 1 purple glitter (cut 1 Star B)
  - 1 gold glitter (cut 1 Star A)
- Gold metallic chenille stem or wired tinsel/cording

Cut chenille stem or wired tinsel/cording to fit finger with some
overlap to twist together. Bend twisted end to flatten against ring.
Glue gold star onto purple star. Glue purple star over twisted area of
ring and use clothespins until dry.

BIRD MASK

PATTERNS ON PAGES 19 & 21

This is great for birthday parties, Halloween, and the first day of spring! It looks especially good with a yellow shirt, yellow pants, and orange socks.

- Art foam (9" x 12" sheets):
  - 1 yellow (cut 1 Basic mask and 1 piece 1" x 2")
  - 1 orange (cut 1 Bird beak)
  - 1 pink (cut 2 Bird cheeks)
- 24" green grosgrain ribbon
- 3½" x 3½" piece of cardboard
- 3" floral wire
- Wood tongue depressor
- 3 yellow boa feathers

Cut out bird eye openings in mask. Glue beak and cheeks to mask. Wrap ribbon around cardboard, slide it off carefully, and secure it tightly in center with floral wire to make a bow. Poke wire into mask ½" from lower edge. Bend wire up and secure in back with a dot of glue. Glue tongue depressor onto back of mask, being sure to cover the floral wire piece. Use fine-tip marker to add an eyebrow above each eye and two ¼" lines for nostrils on beak. Glue three feathers to the back of mask so they stick up at top. Glue the small piece of yellow foam behind feathers to secure them.

PRINCESS MASK

PATTERNS ON PAGES 19 & 30

With this mask you can be Queen or Princess of any land you can imagine, or the star of a Mardi Gras party! Don't forget to be kind t your subjects!

- Art foam (9" x 12" sheets):
  - 1 pink (cut 1 Basic mask and 1 Princess nose)
  - 1 pink glitter (cut 2 Princess cheeks)
  - 1 yellow (cut 1 Princess hair)
  - 1 dark pink (cut 1 Princess lips)
  - 1 gold glitter (cut 1 Princess crown)
- Wood tongue depressor
- Assorted rhinestones

Cut out princess eye openings in mask. Glue hair, nose, cheeks, and lips to mask. Glue crown to hair. Glue rhinestones to crown as desired. Glue various rhinestone shapes to crown. Use fine-tip marker to add all lines on mask, hair, and lips. Glue tongue depressor to bottom of mask, leaving 3" showing.

DOG MASK

PATTERNS ON PAGES 19 & 33

Team up with a friend in the kitten mask, or do your own puppy thing. Put the bow under the chin for a boy dog or at the top of the head for a girl dog.

Art foam (9" x 12" sheets):

- 1 tan (cut 1 Basic mask)
- 1 brown (cut 2 Dog ears)
- 1 ivory (cut 1 Dog muzzle)
- 1 black (cut 1 Dog nose)

20" purple gingham checked ¼" ribbon

2¾" x 2¾" piece of cardboard

2½" piece of floral wire

Wood tongue depressor

Acrylic paint:

- Titanium White
- Lamp Black

Cut out dog eye openings in mask. Glue ears and mouth to mask. Glue nose to muzzle. Paint all details on muzzle and eyebrows Lamp Black. Use Lamp Black and stylus to add dots to muzzle. Paint nose the Titanium White. Wrap ribbon around cardboard, carefully slide it off, and secure tightly in center with floral wire to make a bow. Poke floral wire into top side of mask. Bend wire to be flat against head. Glue on a small piece of tan art foam to cover wire. Glue tongue depressor to bottom of mask, leaving at least 3" showing.

CAT MASK

PATTERNS ON PAGE 31

Expect to hear lots of awwws as you meow your way to people's hearts!

Art foam (9" x 12" sheets):

- 1 gray (cut 1 Cat mask and 2 Cat ears)
- 1 pink (cut 1 Tongue and 2 Cat ear centers)
- 1 black (cut 1 Cat nose)

6 black chenille stems

8" of ⅜" pink grosgrain ribbon

Wood tongue depressor

Acrylic paint:

- Titanium White
- Lamp Black

Cut out cat eye openings in mask. Paint a small Titanium White square on nose. Paint all details on mask and center of ears Lamp Black. Glue pink centers to center of gray ears and glue ears onto top of mask. Glue tongue into point of mouth. Use needle-nosed pliers to cut each chenille stem approximately 3½" long and glue onto mask for whiskers. Tie a bow with the ribbon and glue between ears at top of mask. Glue tongue depressor to bottom of mask, leaving at least 3" showing.

AFRICAN TRIBAL MASK

PATTERNS ON PAGE 30

If you don't know much about the history of African tribes, this is a great time to learn. Make the mask as shown, or do some research and make it match one that was used in real tribal ceremonies.

- Art foam (9" x 12" sheets):
  - 1 zebra print (cut 1 Tribal mask)
  - 1 tiger print (cut 1 Tribal lips, 1 Tribal nose, and 2 Tribal eyelids)
- 3 wood tongue depressors
- Gold, black, and orange glitter writers
- 4½" black beaded trim

Cut out tribal eye and mouth openings in mask. Glue eyelids to top of eye openings and lips around mouth opening. Glue on nose and trim. Use glitter to outline bottom edge of eyelids with gold; eyelids with orange; and nose and inside of mouth black. Apply orange dots around eye and eyelid and black dots outside mouth. On back, glue tongue depressor going straight down from mouth opening. Glue two tongue depressors along lower sides of back to support the mask.

SAILBOAT

PATTERNS ON PAGE 29

Put your name on the side of this boat and sail along on your dreams in the play mat's lake. Better yet, get a friend to make one too and race each other!

- Art foam (9" x 12" sheets):
  - 1 white (cut 1 of Sails)
  - 1 red (cut 1 Flag)
  - 1 tan (cut 2 Decks)
  - 1 brown (cut 2 Hulls)
- 6 black ¼" buttons
- 1 white drinking straw

Glue three buttons onto top section of sailboat. Glue top and bottom sections of sailboat together. Cut straw to a length of 5" and glue to center of one side of sailboat. Glue sails onto straw ⅝" from top. Glue flag to top of straw. Glue remaining side over straw and glue to ends of sails. Do not glue ends of brown section together. Use marker to add "USA" or your name to side of boat on brown section.

PLAY MAT

PATTERNS ON PAGES 28 & 32

Use this play mat with cars, trucks, boats, and trains you made yourself or bought. Add more roads, railroads, or ponds if you want to.

- Art foam (12" x 18" sheets):
  - 4 green
  - 1 brown (cut 4 strips 3" x 18" for roads)
  - 1 (9" x 12" sheet) blue glitter (cut 1 Pond)
  - 1 black (cut 1 Racetrack and many ⁹⁄₁₆" x 12" strips)
- Sewing machine with green thread OR green duct tape

Sew or tape together four sheets of green foam to create a 24" x 3[6]" mat. Glue brown road strips over stitching or use duct tape. Trim any excess to make roads even with outer edges of mat. Glue four ⁹⁄₁₆" x12" strips across the short way 1⅜" apart to form tracks. Cut remaining strips into 3" rails and glue approximately ¾" apart acro[ss] tracks. Glue lake and race track onto mat.

MOVING TRUCK

PATTERNS ON PAGE 22

It's moving day for the play mat neighborhood, and this helpful vehicle has everything under control.

- Art foam (9" x 12" sheets):
  - 1 gray (cut 2 Truck Sides)
  - 1 black (cut 6 Wheels)
  - 1 chartreuse green (cut 2 Truck cabs and 2 Moving bumpers)
  - 1 blue (cut 4 Hubcaps)
  - 1 yellow (cut 2 Moving headlights)
- 1⅛" foam glitter sticker letters
- 2 wood blocks ½" x ½"
- Acrylic paint:
  - Slate Gray
  - Lamp Black
  - Sour Apple

Paint Lamp Black lines on truck cab and "Moving" (and your name, if desired in place of foam letters) onto truck box area. Paint one wood block Slate Gray and one Sour Apple. Adhere foam letters to truck box area. Glue truck cab to box. Glue Sour Apple block between cab and Slate Gray block between box section so truck will stand. Glue hubcaps to wheels. Glue wheels to truck, making sure they are even so the truck will stand upright. Glue headlights to front of truck. Glue bumpers to rear of truck.

TRAIN AND SIGN

PATTERNS ON PAGE 27

Choo-choo! Make your way down the play mat track with this train, and use the railroad crossing sign to make sure everyone knows you're coming!

- Art foam (9" x 12" sheets):
  - 1 black (cut 2 Trains and 2 Train Hubcaps)
  - 1 gray (cut 2 Smokestacks)
  - 1 tan (cut 2 pieces ¼" x 1¾" for roofs; cut 2 Cow catchers)
  - 1 yellow (cut 2 Train Lights)
  - 1 brown (cut 4 Train Wheels)
  - 1 white (cut 2 pieces ½" by 2" for sign)
- 2 wood blocks ½" x ½"
- 2" wood axle
- 1⅛" wood spool
- Acrylic paint: Lamp Black

Paint both wood blocks, wood axle, and wood spool Lamp Black. Use fine-tip marker to print "crossing" on one white strip. Glue two white strips together in an X, with "crossing" on top. Print "rail road" on back strip. Use broad-tip marker to add lines to cow catcher. On each side, glue on train roof, smoke stack, cow catcher, and light. Glue black wood block between bodies so the train stands. Glue hubcaps to wheels and wheels to train body. Make sure they are even so the train stands upright. Glue axle into hole of spool. Glue railroad sign to axle.

RACE CAR

PATTERNS ON PAGE 22

If you want to vrooooooom your way around the neighborhood, this race car is the vehicle for you.

- Art foam (9" x 12" sheets):
  - 1 yellow (cut 2 Race Cars)
  - 1 black (cut 4 Wheels and 1 Seat)
  - 1 orange (cut 4 Hubcaps)
- 2 wood blocks ½" x ½"
- Acrylic paint: Yellow Light
- Blue dimensional paint: Calypso Blue

Paint both blocks Yellow Light. Glue seat to each car body. Glue blocks between the bodies so the car stands. Glue hubcaps to wheels. Glue two wheels to each side of car body. Make sure they are even so it will stand upright. Use dimensional paint to add a racing stripe and your age.

CAR

PATTERNS ON PAGE 22

Hop your imagination into this car and zip around on the roads of the play mat. Who knows where your journey will end?

- Art foam (9" x 12" sheets):
  - 1 red (cut 2 Cars)
  - 1 yellow (cut 2 Headlights)
  - 1 orange (cut 2 Tail lights)
  - 1 gray (cut 4 Bumpers)
  - 1 black (cut 4 Wheels)
- 4 white ¼" buttons
- 4 red ⅜" buttons
- 2 wood blocks ½" x ½"
- Acrylic paint: Cherry Red

Use ruler and fine-tip marker to add door lines. Paint both wood blocks Cherry Red. Glue tail light, headlight, and bumpers to each car body side. Make sure the sides across from each other line up properly. Glue painted blocks between bodies so car will stand. Glue wheels onto car body. Make sure all wheels are even so the car stands upright. Glue on buttons for door handles and center of wheels.

BARN

PATTERNS ON PAGES 24 & 25

This barn is just the right size for your animals and tractor, and the doors even open so things can pass through.

- Art foam (9" x 12" sheets):
  - 1 red (cut 1 Barn)
  - 1 black (cut 1 Barn Window)
  - 1 yellow (cut 1 Straw)
  - 1 gray (cut 4 Hinges)
  - 1 white (cut 2 Barn Doors)
  - 1 green (cut 1 Barn Roof)
- 2 black ⅝" buttons
- 4 wood blocks ¾" x ¾"
- 2 wood craft sticks
- Acrylic paint: Cherry Red

Paint blocks and craft sticks Cherry Red. Use fine-point marker and ruler to draw straw, board, and wood grain lines. Glue roof and window to barn, straw to window, hinges to barn and doors, and buttons to doors. On back of barn, glue two blocks on top of each other on each side of barn doors so it stands by itself. Glue craft sticks above blocks.

TRACTOR

PATTERNS ON PAGES 24 & 25

Putt-putt-putt-putt—every farm needs a tractor! Create it in green, red, blue, or your favorite tractor color.

- Art foam (9" x 12" sheets):
  - 1 green (cut 2 Tractors)
  - 1 yellow (cut 2 each Tractor front hubcaps and Tractor back hubcaps)
  - 1 black (cut 2 each, Tractor windows, Tractor front tires, and Tractor back tires)
- Acrylic pain: Festive Green
- 2 wood blocks ½" x ½"

Paint both wood blocks Festive Green. Glue wood blocks between tractor pieces so it stands. Glue windows to tractor, hubcaps to wheels, and wheels to tractor. Make sure the wheels are even so the tractor stands upright. Glue tops of tractor together.

TREE

PATTERN ON PAGE 28

To show a tree in autumn, use red, orange, or yellow instead of green for the leaves and skip the apples.

- Art foam (9" x 12" sheets):
  - 1 green (cut 2 Trees)
  - 1 red
  - 1 brown
- Empty toilet paper roll

Measure toilet paper roll and cut brown art foam to fit. Glue foam to roll, using clothespins until glue dries. Use large hole punch to punch ¼" circles out of red foam and glue to the green tree section. Glue green tree section to top of brown tube on both sides. Glue top of tree together.

PIG

PATTERNS ON PAGE 27

Here, piggy! Is this the littlest pig or the one that went to market? The decision is yours.

Art foam (9" x 12" sheets):

- 1 pink (cut 1 each, Pig body, Pig head, Pig nose, and Animal stand)
- 1 green chartreuse

1½" pink chenille stem

Acrylic paint: Lamp Black

Paint eyebrows, ear marks, and nostrils Lamp Black. Use stylus and Lamp Black to dot on eyes. Curl chenille stem around pencil and glue to upper rear section of body. Glue two body sections together. Glue nose to head and head to body. Cut V's into chartreuse art foam piece for grass. Glue grass to each side of slit. Insert stand into slit.

CHICKEN

PATTERNS ON PAGES 26 & 27

Here chick, chick, chick! This chicken doesn't give you eggs, but will put a smile to your face!

- Art foam (9" x 12" sheets):
  - 1 white (cut 1 each of Chicken head, Chicken body, Chicken back, and Animal stand)
  - 1 yellow (cut 1 Chicken beak)
  - 1 red (cut 1 Chicken comb)
  - 1 chartreuse green
- 1 white boa feather

Glue comb to back of head, bill to front of head, head to body, back to body, and feather to back. Use fine-tip marker to dot in two eyes and add eyebrows and nostrils. Insert stand into slit. Cut V's into green strip for grass and glue to base of chicken on each side of slit.

CAT

PATTERNS ON PAGES 26 & 27

Here kitty, kitty! This kitty is so friendly to have around your farm and so good at chasing away mice.

Art foam (9" x 12" sheets):

- 1 gray (cut 1 each, Cat head, Cat body, and Animal stand)
- 1 chartreuse green

4" of ⅛" pink satin ribbon

Acrylic paint:

- Bubblegum Pink
- Lamp Black

Use fine-tip marker to draw ears, eyebrows, eyes, nose, mouth, and whiskers on the head. Paint the inside of ears Bubblegum Pink and eyebrows, mouth, and whiskers Lamp Black. Use stylus and Lamp Black to dot on eyes. Glue head to body. Insert stand into slit. Clip V's from green art foam strip for grass and glue to each side of slit.

SHEEP

PATTERNS ON PAGES 26 & 27

Baaaaa! This wooly sheep is a little wild, but very friendly. You'll enjoy having him on your farm.

- Art foam (9" x 12" sheets):
  - 1 white (cut 1 each, Sheep body and Animal stand)
  - 1 black (cut 1 Sheep head)
  - 1 chartreuse green
- ½" white button
- Acrylic paint: Titanium White

Use stylus and Titanium White to dot on eyes. Paint white eyebrows. Use fine-tip marker to draw curls on front and back of body. Glue button to head and head to body. Insert stand into slit. Cut V's into green art foam piece for grass and glue to each side of slit.

EASTER EGG IN HOLDER

This Easter egg in its own holder is the perfect decoration or gift to celebrate the holiday with. Make it even more special by writing the year and each person's name on his or her egg.

- Art foam (9" x 12" sheets):
  - 1 white (cut 1¼" x 6¾")
  - 1 yellow (cut ⅜" x 6¾")
  - Scrap pieces of pink, lavender, and light green (each at least 1" x 1")
- 2½" wood egg (or use a real hard-boiled egg)
- Acrylic paint:
  - Bubblegum Pink
  - Marigold
  - Purple Cow
  - Sour Apple
  - Titanium White

Measure your egg to be sure you have enough white and yellow art foam for the egg stand. Use large hole punch to make ¼" circles from scrap pieces of art foam in various colors. Glue punched circles on yellow strip. Glue yellow strip to center of white strip. Overlap ½" and glue ends together to form a circle. Before glue dries, make sure egg will sit in stand. Use clothespins until dry. Paint egg Titanium White. It may take 3 to 4 coats; let it dry completely between them. Use a pencil to draw a ⅝" strip vertically around egg. Paint the strip Marigold. Again, it may take several coats. Dot Bubblegum Pink, Purple Cow, and Sour Apple on strip.

LADYBUG PLACEMAT

PATTERNS ON PAGES 20 & 33

Bring ladybugs and dragonflies to the table on this fun placemat. Make enough for all your guests.

- Art foam (9" x 12" sheets):
  - 1 (12" x 18" sheet) green
  - 1 white (cut 6 Dragonflies)
  - 1 black (cut 6 Thorax B's, 1 Ladybug head, 3 Ladybug spots, and 1 Ladybug stripe)
  - 1 red (cut 1 Ladybug body)
- Glitter paint: Ice Crystal
- Acrylic paint: Sour Apple
- 3½" of 18 gauge copper wire

Paint Ice Crystal onto dragonfly. Dot Sour Apple eyes onto thorax. Glue thorax on top of dragonfly. Use needle-nosed pliers to bend copper wire into a U-shape. Poke one end of wire into top of head. Bend ends into a circle. Glue ladybug head, stripe, and dots to body. Glue ladybug to center of placemat. Glue three dragonflies to each side of placemat.

DRAGONFLY CUP HOLDER

PATTERNS ON PAGE 20

This cup holder can be made to fit any size of cup. It's easy to personalize the holder by writing a name on it.

- Art foam (9" x 12" sheets):
  - 1 (or size around glass/cup) lavender
  - 1 white (cut 4 Dragonflies)
  - 1 black (cut 4 Thorax B's)
- Acrylic paint: Sour Apple
- Glitter paint: Ice Crystal

Dot Sour Apple eyes onto each thorax. Paint Ice Crystal over entire wing surface. Glue thorax on top of wings. Glue dragonflies onto cup holder.

SPORT SCHEDULE HOLDER

PATTERNS ON PAGE 34

This sports activity magnet is just what you need to keep track of all your games and practices!

Art foam (9" x 12" sheets):

- 1 (12" x 18" sheet) royal blue (cut 5" x 18")
- 1 white (cut 1 Soccer ball, 1 Baseball, and 1 Football stripe)
- 1 cream (cut 1 Baseball bat)
- 1 light brown (cut 1 Football)
- 1 orange (cut 1 Basketball)
- 1 brown
- 1 green (cut 1 Sports flag)
- 2 gold glitter stars (1½" pre-cut or cut Star B's)
- 1 blue glitter star (1½" pre-cut or cut Star B's)
- 4 gold glitter stars (1" pre-cut or cut Star A's)
- 2 blue glitter stars (1" pre-cut or cut Star A's)
- 4 gold glitter stars (¾" pre-cut or cut Star A's large)

⅝" foam sticker letters

3 wood clip-style 1¾" clothespins

4½" x 13½" magnetic adhesive sheet

Acrylic paint:

- Lamp Black
- Cherry Red

Paint Lamp Black lines on balls and bat. Paint center and half diamond shapes on outer edges Lamp Black. Glue brown art foam for pennant's stick on end. Add name to pennant. Glue magnet sheet to back side of blue art foam. Glue white strips to each end of football. Glue one clothespin in center of blue art foam along lower edge and remaining two clothespins approximately 2-inches from each side edge. Glue on pennant and sport items. Glue glitter stars on clothespins. Add remaining glitter stars around pennant and sports items.

COW

(PICTURED ON PAGE 12)

PATTERNS ON PAGES 26 & 27

Moooooo! This cow is ruler of this farm and has the attitude to show it.

- Art foam (9" x 12" sheets):
  - 1 white (cut 1 each, Cow head, Cow body, and Animal stand)
  - 1 black (cut 2 Spots)
  - 1 pink (cut 1 Cow nose and 2 Cow ears)
  - 1 chartreuse green
- Acrylic paint:
  - Bubblegum Pink
  - Lamp Black
- Black buttons:
  - ¾"
  - 1"

Use fine-tip marker to draw face, nose, and ear details. Paint inner section of ear Bubblegum Pink and eyebrows and nostrils Lamp Black. Dot on black eyes. Glue nose to head, head to body, spots to front and back of body, large button to end of tail, and small button to top of head. Insert stand into slit. Clip V's from green art foam strip for grass and glue to each side of body slit.

FIRECRACKER HAT

PATTERNS ON PAGES 23 & 33

This fits-any-size hat is just the thing to celebrate the 4th of July, Veteran's Day, or any holiday that could use some sparkle and pizzazz. If you don't live in the United States, just adjust the colors and lettering to reflect your own country.

- Art foam (9" x 12" sheets):
  - 1 white (cut 1 Candle)
  - 1 red (cut 1 Candle and 1 Star C)
  - 1 blue (cut 1 Candle and 1 Star C)
  - 1 (12" x 18" sheet) Black (1¼" x around head of wearer)
- 3 gold metallic 1½" chenille stems
- Dimensional paint: gold glitter
- 3 glitter 1¼" poms
- 1⅛" glitter sticker letters
- 3 wood 2½" craft sticks
- Acrylic paint:
  - Cherry Red
  - Ocean Blue
  - Titanium White

Slightly round corners of three candles. Glue on chenille stems. Glue glitter poms on stems. Paint one wood craft stick Cherry Red, one Ocean Blue, and one Titanium White. When dry, glue to back of candles. Glue ends of hatband together. Use clothespins until dry. Glue firecrackers to front of headband. Press on glitter letters. Outline stars with gold glitter and glue on hat.

BUNNY EASTER BASKET

PATTERNS ON PAGE 27

This is an easy way to decorate a plain basket for Easter. Just add Easter grass and fill it with candy or cookies for dessert.

- Art foam (9" x 12" sheets):
  - 1 white (cut 6 Bunny heads and 12 Bunny ears)
  - 1 pink (cut 12 Bunny inside ears)
  - 1 gray (punch 6 circles ¼")
- ¼" satin picot ribbon
  - 1¼ yard yellow
  - 1½ yard mint green
  - 1¼ yard purple
- 4" x 5" piece of cardboard
- Basket approximately 4" x 6" x 8"
- ³⁄₁₆" wiggly eyes
- Acrylic paint: Lamp Black

Glue gray circles onto heads as noses. Glue wiggly eyes above nose. Paint a ¼" Lamp Black line down from each nose and eyebrows above each eye. Glue pink centers to each ear. Glue two ears to each head. Use 6" of each picot ribbon color to make a bow and glue it between the ears. Glue rabbits evenly around basket. Cut a 6" piece of mint green ribbon. Wrap remaining ribbons around cardboard, slide off carefully, and use green ribbon to secure tightly in center, creating a bow. Tie onto center of basket handle.

VALENTINE EYEGLASSES

PATTERNS ON PAGE 29

These funny Love Specs are so fun to wear! See if guests at your Valentine party can tell who you are behind them.

- Art foam (9" x 12" sheets):
  - 1 red (cut 2 Heart F's and 1 piece ⅜" x 1½")
  - 1 white (cut 2 Heart C's)
  - 1 pink (cut 2 Heart B's)
- 2 gold metallic chenille stems
- Glitter paint: Ice Crystal
- Foam or dimensional paint:
  - White
  - Hot Pink
  - Red

Cut out centers of red hearts. Use foam or dimensional paint to outline large hearts with White and Hot Pink; white hearts with Hot Pink; and red hearts with Red. Paint Ice Crystal on all hearts. Glue hearts together as shown. Use a hole punch to make a hole to insert chenille stems. Glue strip of red foam between two large hearts for nosepiece; measure between eyes to have enough space between hearts and fit comfortably on bridge of nose. Push chenille stem through hole from back and curl a couple times around a pencil to keep ear piece from pulling out. Bend end of chenille stem to form over ear.

VALENTINE BIRDIE BOX

PATTERNS ON PAGES 20, 31 & 32

Valentines are even more fun when you have a special box to keep them in. This box is big enough that it might hold several years' worth of valentines!

- Art foam (9" x 12" sheets):
- 1 (12" x 18" sheet) white (will cover almost any size tissue box)
- 1 light pink (cut 8 Heart B's)
- 1 (12" x 18" sheet) pink (cut 1 Head, 2 Heart F's, and 10 Heart B's)
- 1 white (cut 2 Heart B's)
- 1 yellow (cut 2 Beaks)
- 1 red (cut 2 Heart D's)
- 2 wiggly ¼" eyes
- Empty box of facial tissues
- 3 pink boa feathers
- 3 pink chenille stems (cut into five 4"-long pieces)
- Decorative trim—measure around tissue box to determine amount needed

Cut foam to fit tissue box and glue on. Glue light pink heart to end of each stem. Twist stems and feathers together into tail and glue to box. Glue one large pink heart over tail chenille ends. Glue on eyes and beaks. Use fine-tip marker to draw eyebrows. Glue 3 light pink hearts to head and neck. Use knife to lightly score (cut partway through foam) ¼" from neck edge. Fold along scored line and glue to box. To support head, cut a ¼" x 4" white art foam strip to glue on opposite side of fold. Lightly score ¼" from large pink heart points. Glue red heart and white heart to large pink heart. Glue the score line on both hearts to sides of box. Adhere trim to top edge of box.

VALENTINE CARD

PATTERNS ON PAGES 20, 29 & 31

Everyone loves to get a Valentine card, especially if the sender made the card personally! This clever card has an added treat.

- Art foam (9" x 12" sheets):
  - 1 fuchsia glitter (cut 1 of Heart F)
  - 1 pink (cut 2 Heart D's)
  - 1 white (cut 1 Heart B)
- Stick of chewing gum
- Envelope 3⅝" x 6½"
- Acrylic paint: Lamp Black
- Dimensional pain: gold glitter

Paint lettering Lamp Black. Use gold glitter to outline the white and pink hearts. Use knife to cut two slits on glitter heart. Slip a stick of chewing gum into the slit. Glue pink and white hearts to glitter heart.

TROPICAL WINDSOCK

PATTERNS ON PAGES 21 & 28

Create a tropical windsock to enjoy yourself or give as a gift. It's a great reminder of how much fun it is to be at the ocean!

- Art foam (12" x 18" sheets):
  - 1 blue (cut 1 piece 7" x 18" and 4 pieces ½" x 1½")
  - 1 chartreuse green (cut 1 Fish D; cut 3 danglers 1¼" x 12"; cut Seaweed)
  - 1 lavender (cut 3 danglers 1¼" x 12")
  - 1 yellow (cut 1 Fish C; cut 3 danglers 1¼" x 12")
- Art foam (9" x 12" sheets):
  - 1 dark green (cut 1 Fins D; cut Seaweed)
  - 1 medium green (cut Seaweed)
  - 1 tan (cut 1 Sand)
  - 1 turquoise (cut 1 Fins C)
  - 1 light pink (cut 1 Fish B)
  - 1 dark pink (cut 1 Fins B)
  - 1 white (cut 1 each Fish Eyes A, B, C, and D)
  - 1 orange (cut 1 Fish A)
  - 1 light orange (cut 1 Fins A)
- Dimensional paint:
  - Brown
  - Green
  - Blue glitter
  - Crystal glitter
  - Green glitter
- Acrylic paint: Lamp Black
- Variety of small seashells
- 3 yards of ¼" chartreuse green satin ribbon

Paint all details on all fish parts Lamp Black. Add details to all leaves, using green between leaves and green glitter for leaf veins. Glue on sand and leaves. Use brown dimensional paint to add lines to sand. Glue seashells on sand. Glue fins, eyes, and tails to fish. Glue on fish. Add bubbles of blue and crystal glitter dots. Glue danglers evenly around bottom of windsock. Glue side seam with a slight overlap. Use clothespins at top and bottom until dry. (Hint: Lay seam side down and put something with some weight to it over the seam to help hold it together until dry.) Use large hole punch to make four ¼" holes evenly along top approximately ⅜" from top edge. Glue small blue strips over holes. Re-punch holes. Cut ribbon into four equal pieces. Loop a ribbon through the hole. Bring loose ends up and tie all together, leaving 4" of ribbon hanging loose. Tie 2 loose ribbons together to create a loop for hanging.

FAIRY DOOR

PATTERNS ON PAGE 33

Create a fairy door to attach to the base of a tree. Pretending fairies are all around us is soothing to the soul!

- Art foam (9" x 12" sheets):
  - 1 light brown (cut 1 Fairy door)
  - 1 yellow (cut 1 Fairy door window)
- ½" gray button

Use ruler to draw board lines on door and dividing lines on yellow window. Glue window and button to door.

X   X

Basic Mask
(CENTER INSIDE OF EYE ON X)

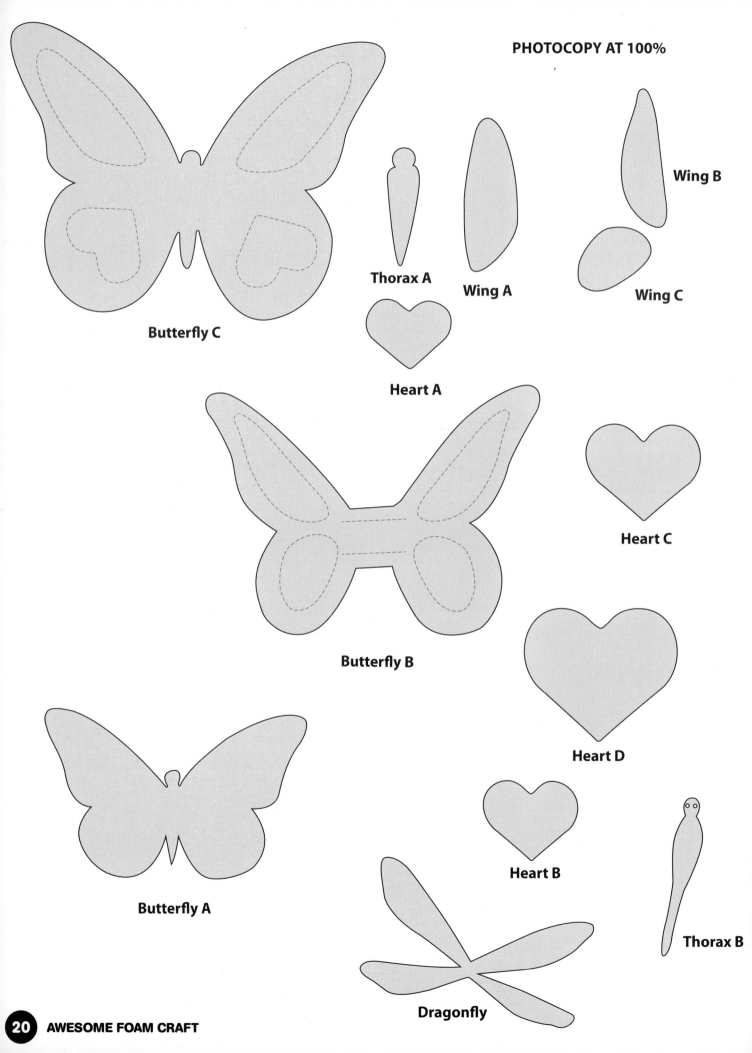

PHOTOCOPY AT 100%

Butterfly C

Thorax A

Wing A

Wing B

Wing C

Heart A

Heart C

Butterfly B

Heart D

Butterfly A

Heart B

Thorax B

Dragonfly

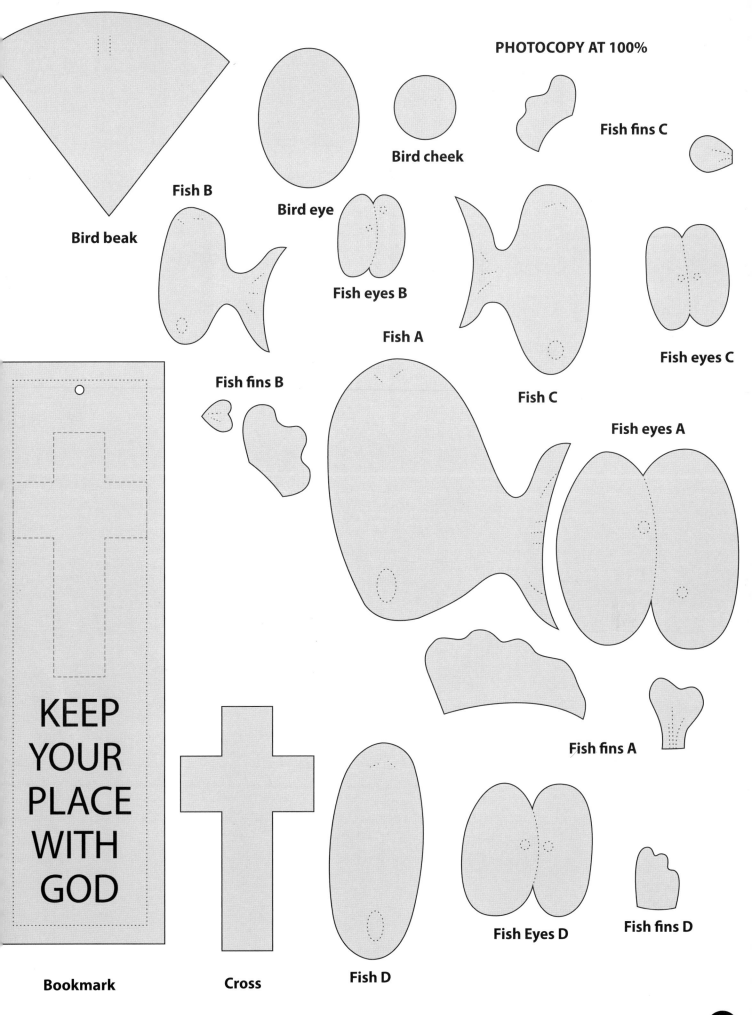

Bird beak

Fish B

Bird eye

Bird cheek

Fish fins C

Fish eyes B

Fish A

Fish eyes C

Fish C

Fish eyes A

Fish fins B

KEEP
YOUR
PLACE
WITH
GOD

Fish fins A

Bookmark

Cross

Fish D

Fish Eyes D

Fish fins D

PHOTOCOPY AT 100%

PHOTOCOPY AT 100%

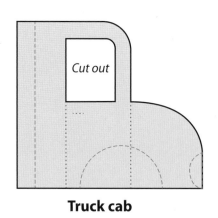

Truck cab

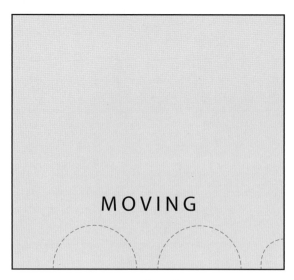

MOVING

Truck side

Moving headlight **Moving bumper**

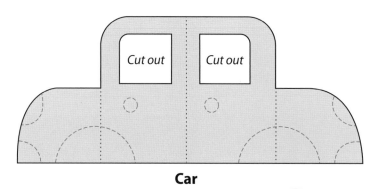

Car

Bumper **Headlight** **Tail light** **Wheel**

Hub cap

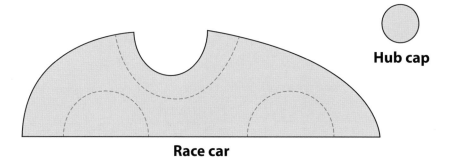

Race car

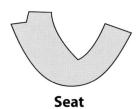

Seat

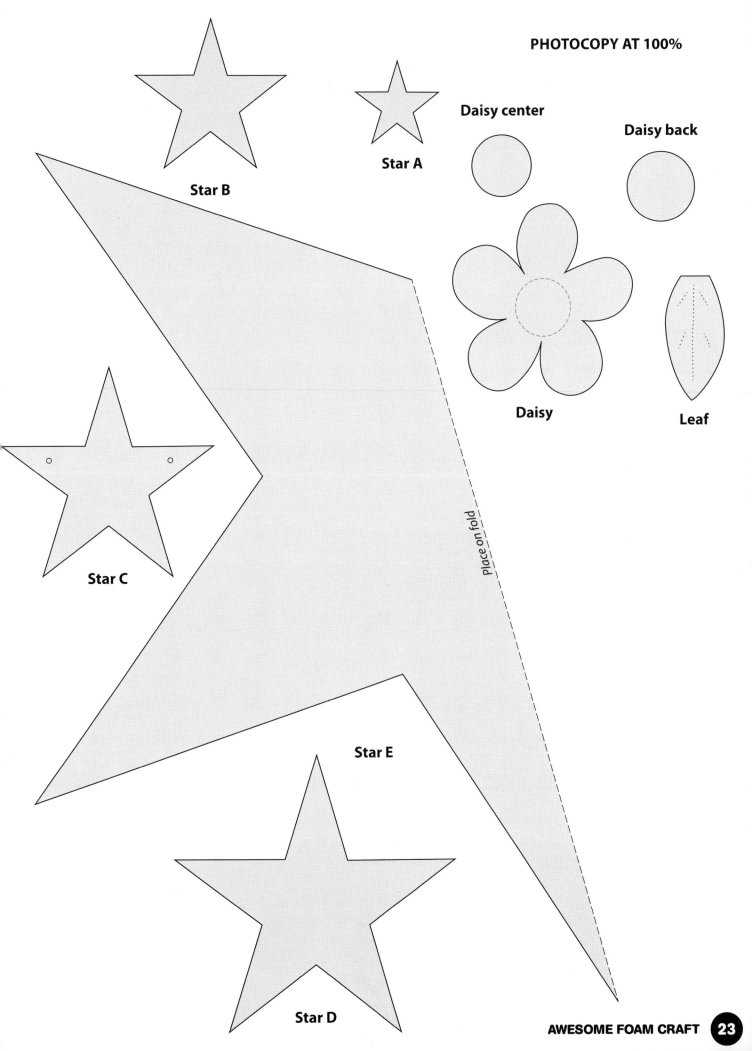

PHOTOCOPY AT 100%

Daisy center

Daisy back

Star A

Star B

Star C

Daisy

Leaf

Place on fold

Star E

Star D

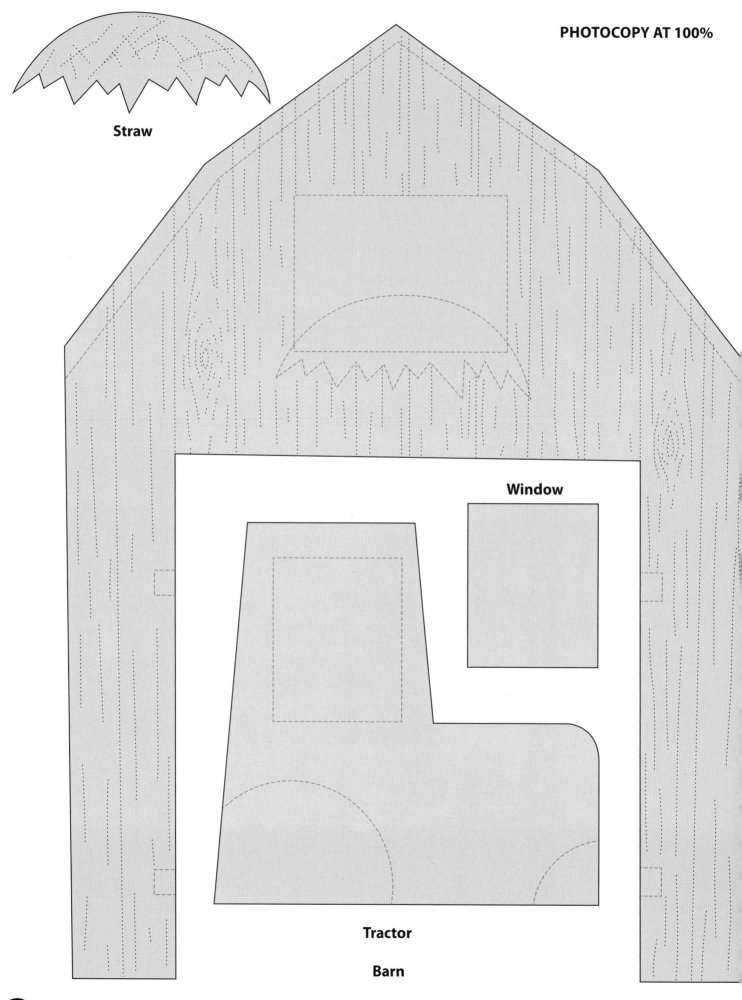

Straw

Window

Tractor

Barn

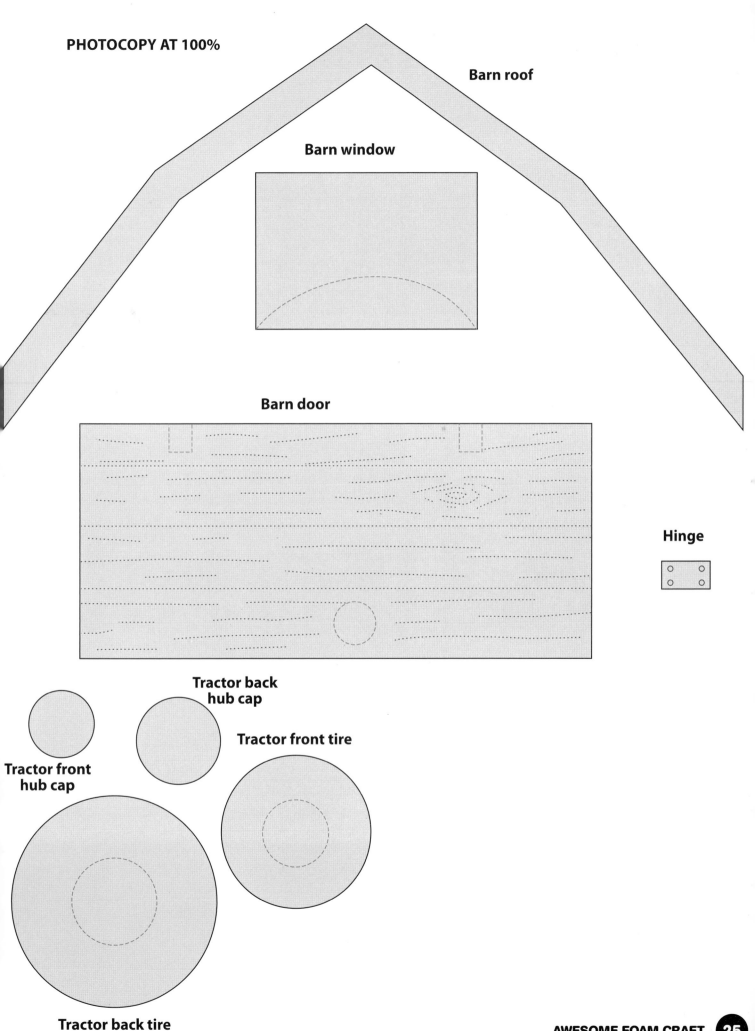

PHOTOCOPY AT 100%

Barn roof

Barn window

Barn door

Hinge

Tractor back
hub cap

Tractor front tire

Tractor front
hub cap

Tractor back tire

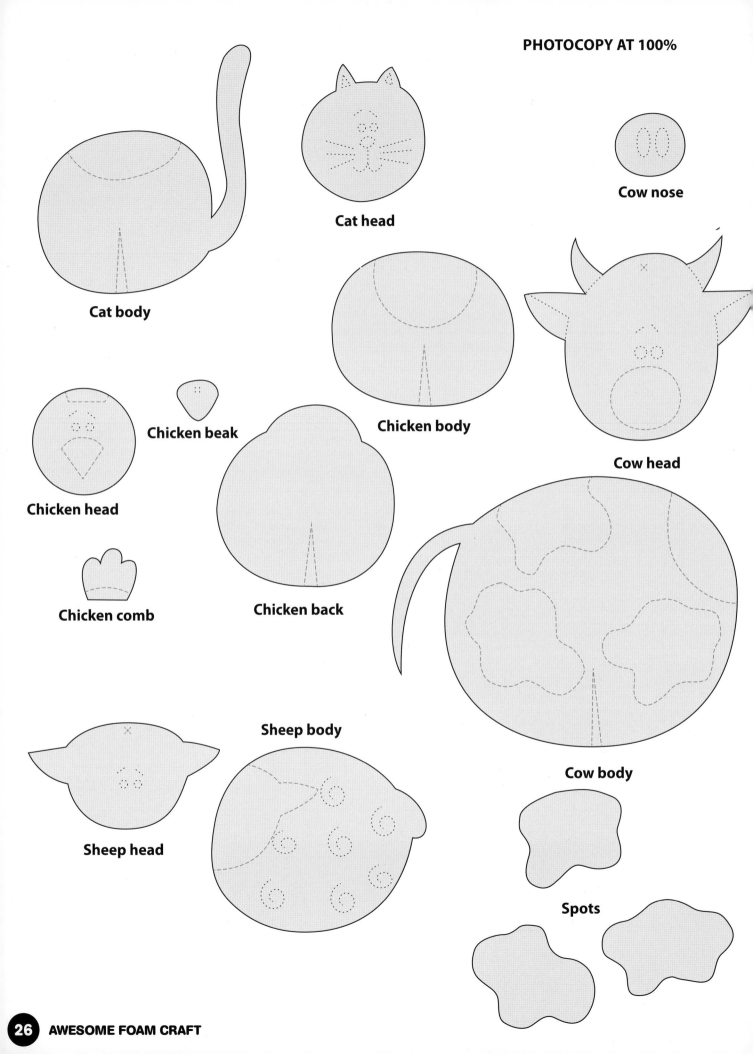

Cow nose

Cat head

Cat body

Chicken beak

Chicken body

Chicken head

Cow head

Chicken comb

Chicken back

Sheep body

Cow body

Sheep head

Spots

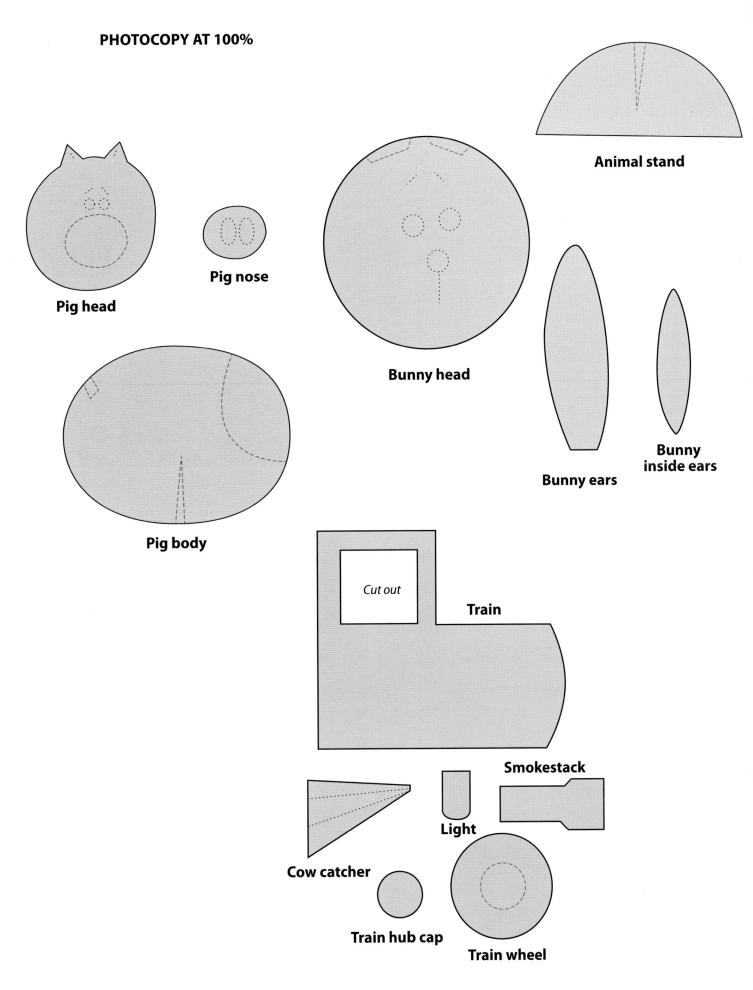

Animal stand

Pig head

Pig nose

Bunny head

Bunny ears

Bunny inside ears

Pig body

Cut out

Train

Smokestack

Light

Cow catcher

Train hub cap

Train wheel

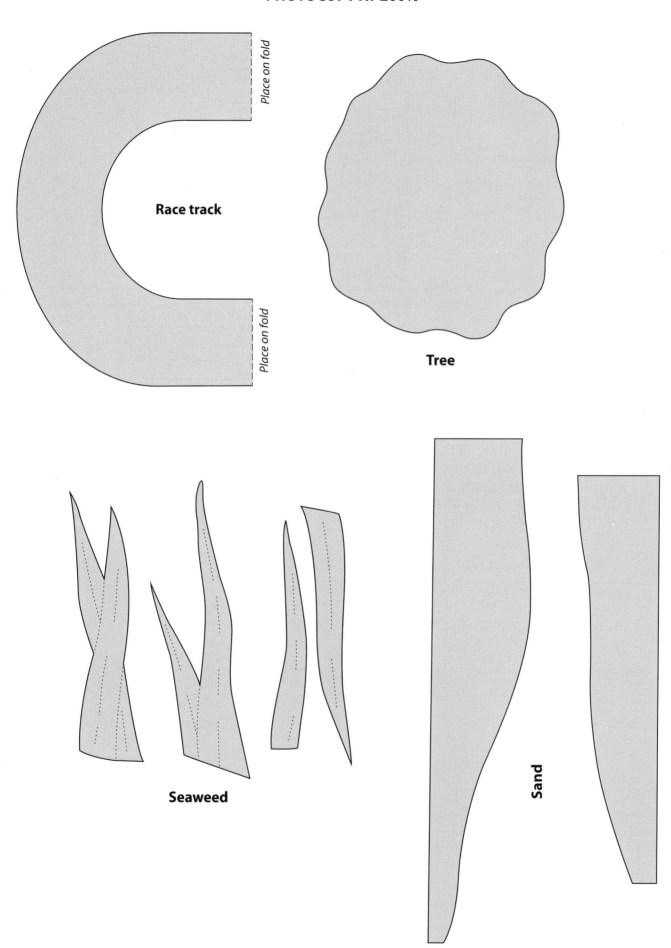

Race track

Place on fold

Place on fold

Tree

Seaweed

Sand

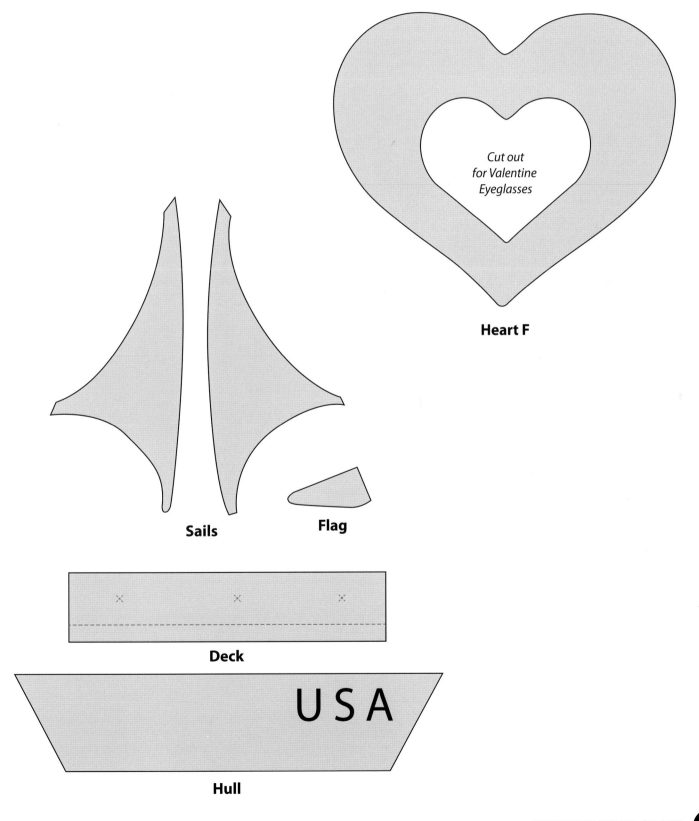

*Cut out
for Valentine
Eyeglasses*

Heart F

Sails

Flag

Deck

USA

Hull

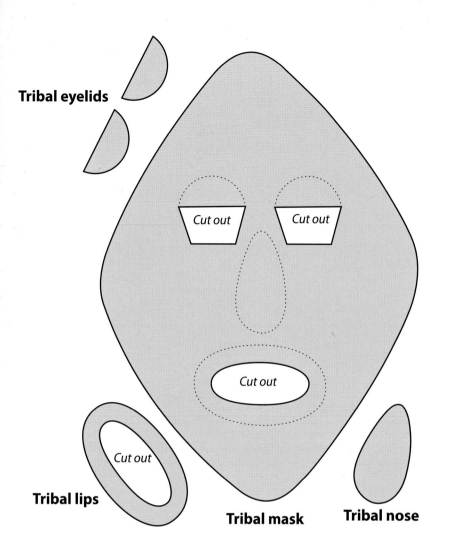

Tribal eyelids

Cut out

Cut out

Cut out

Tribal lips

Cut out

Tribal mask

Tribal nose

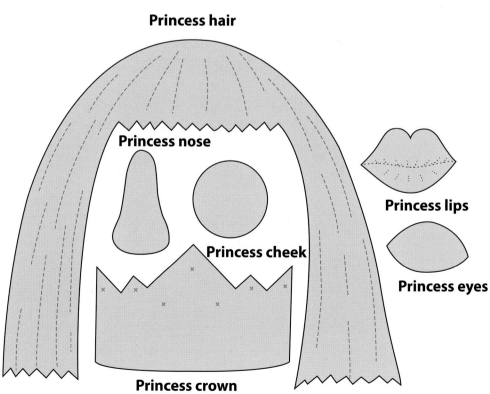

Princess hair

Princess nose

Princess cheek

Princess lips

Princess eyes

Princess crown

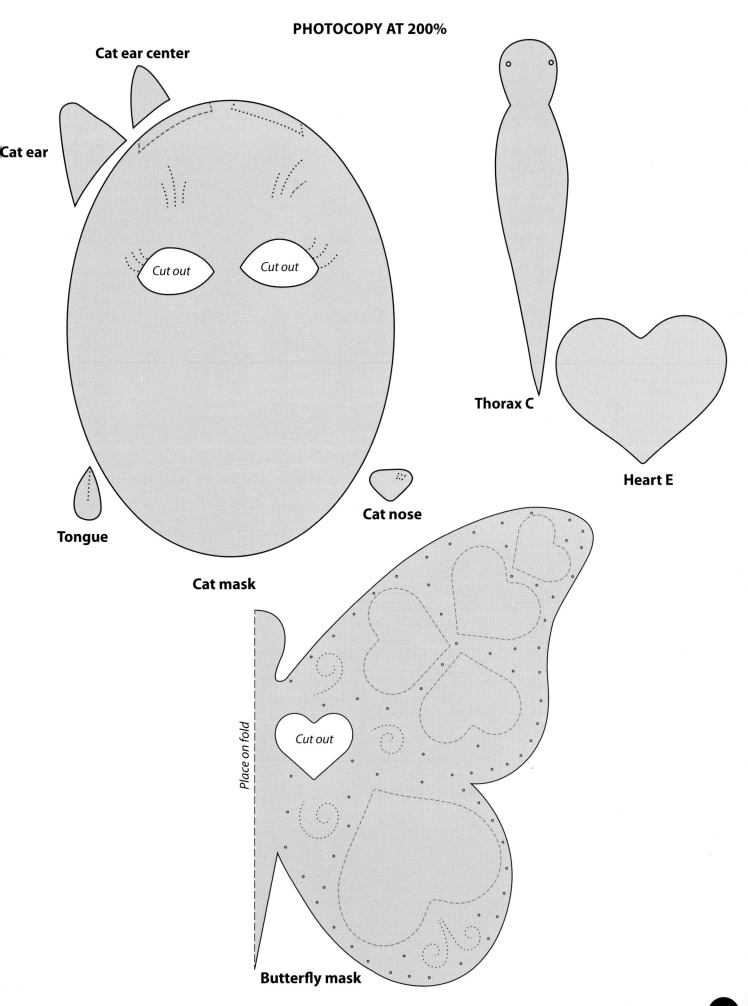

PHOTOCOPY AT 200%

Cat ear center

Cat ear

Cut out

Cut out

Tongue

Cat mask

Cat nose

Thorax C

Heart E

Place on fold

Cut out

Butterfly mask

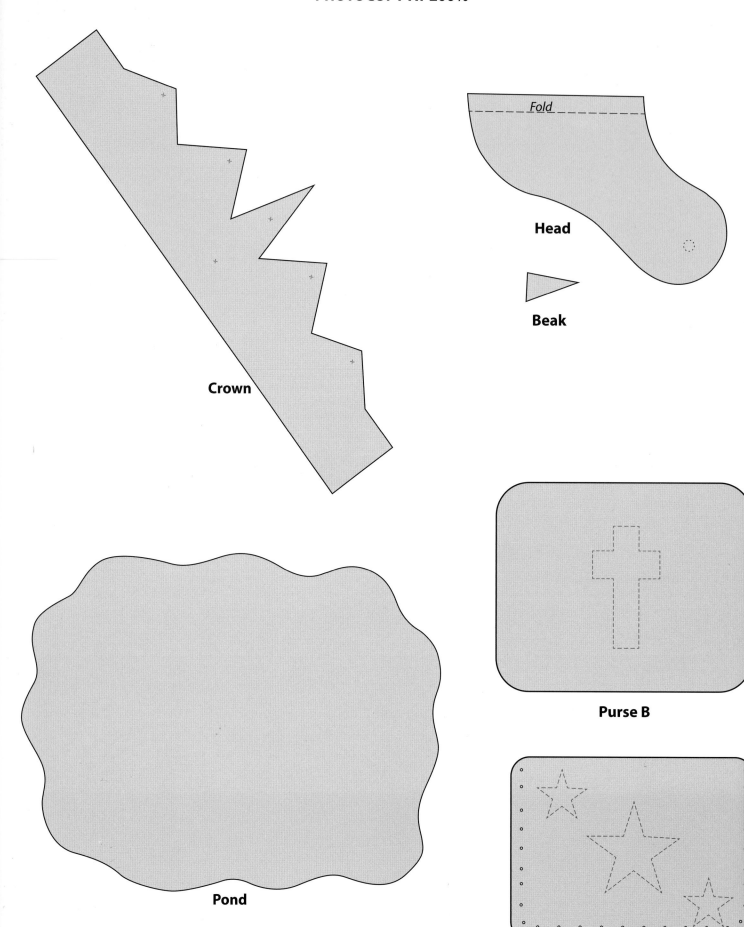

Crown

Head

Beak

Pond

Purse B

Purse A

Fold

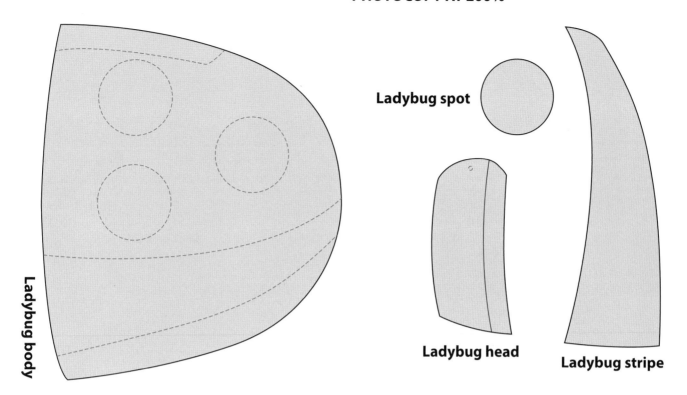

Ladybug spot

Ladybug body

Ladybug head

Ladybug stripe

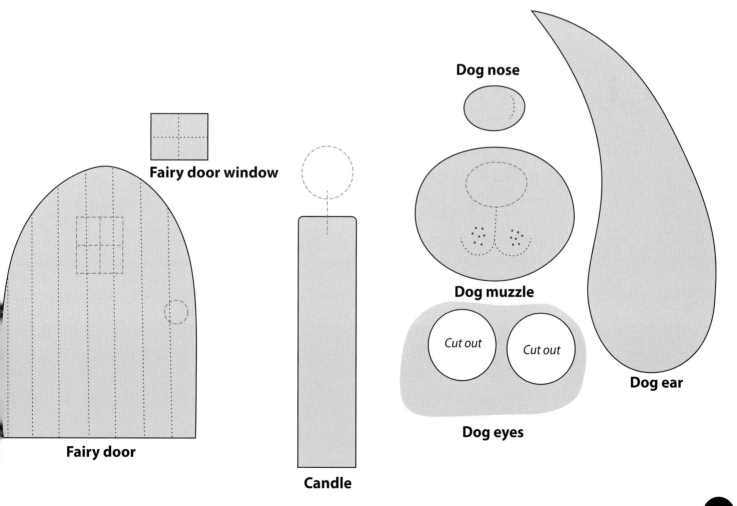

Fairy door window

Fairy door

Candle

Dog nose

Dog muzzle

Cut out   *Cut out*

Dog eyes

Dog ear

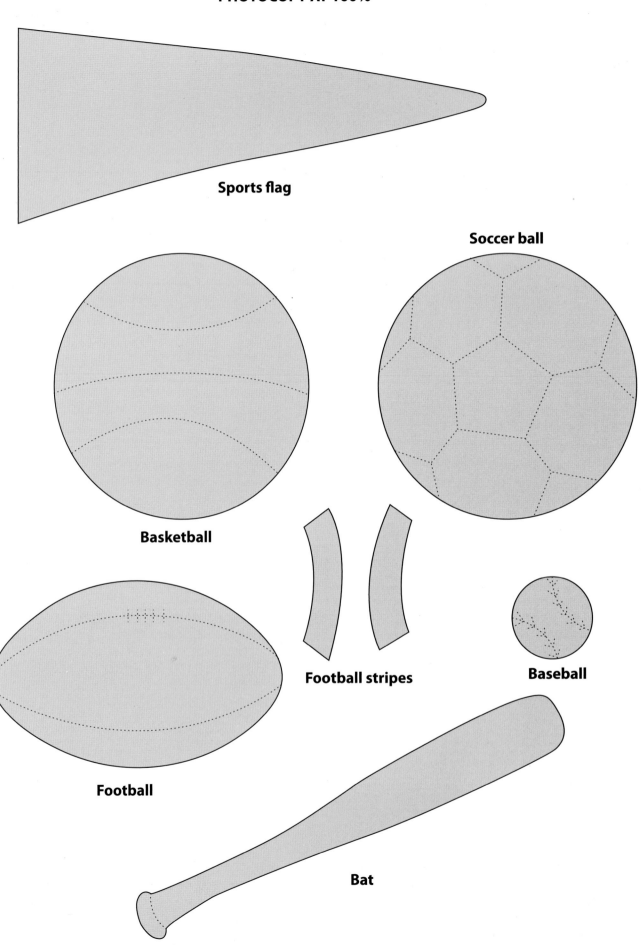

Sports flag

Soccer ball

Basketball

Football stripes

Baseball

Football

Bat